BE THAT EMPTY

Apologia for Air

Alice B. Fogel

Harbor Mountain Press
Brownsville, Vermont

Harbor Mountain Press acknowledges the support of
Pentangle Council on the Arts (Woodstock, Vermont)
for this and other literary projects.

First printing 2007

ISBN 0-9786009-2-4

Series Editor
Peter Money

Production editing
Barbara Jones

Cover image
© Susan Osgood
www.vermontgalleries.com/osgood/

Harbor Mountain Press
Brownsville, Vermont
0 5 0 3 7
www.harbormountainpress.com

ACKNOWLEDGMENTS

Alligator Juniper— "Shapeshifters" (First Prize, "Nature and Psyche" competition)

Barrow Street— "Scissors"

Blue Ink— "Again"

Blueline— "Moorings" (as "The Mooring")

The Boston Globe— "Clay Babies"

Chelsea— "Sweet Vein" (as "Sweeter Than Life"); "Shed Light"

Crab Creek Review— "Old Diary"

Cream City Review— "Anticipation"

Frisk Magazine—"Missing"

Fugue— "Starting Small"

Green Mountains Review— "To the Bone"; "Disturbance"

Heartbeat of New England: Anthology of Contemporary Nature Poetry— "Anticipation"

Hootenanny: Magazine of Art and Literature—"The Gift" (illustrated by Fran Beallor)

Hubbub— "Homing"

The Journal— "The Eye"

The Larcom Review— "From Some Notes on Longing" (as "Longing"); "After Sleep"

Many Mountains Moving— "The Gift"

Marlboro Review— "Map of a Distant Land"

No Tell Motel—"Hearts"

Notre Dame Review—"The Leaf"

(NDR's website also features "Sweet Vein" and "Shapeshifters")

Phoebe— "Generation"; "Stranded"

Pleiades— After Marc Chagall: "Bridges"; "Bella"; "Uprooted"; "Blue Soul" (also First Honorable Mentions, Eve of St. Agnes Award from *Negative Capability*)

Poetica—"God's Body"

Poetry Daily—"The Owl"

Quantum Tao—"Geologic Time"

Rattapallax—"Trompe L'Oeil"

Red Brick Review—"Fractured Lullaby" (as "Rainbow Person Box")

Seedhouse—"Word"

Southern Poetry Review—"Devotion"; "Killing Frost"; "In Summer Night"

Tar River Poetry—"Degrees of Gratitude"

The 2008 Poets' Guide to New Hampshire—"Sweet Vein"

TriQuarterly—"The Owl"

Under the Legislature of Stars: An Anthology of NH Poets—"Starting Small"

Victory Park—"No Witness" (in its earlier, sonnet form); "White on White"; "God's Body"

Wavelength—"Interior With Painter's Wife"; "Evolution"

Many of these poems have been changed since their appearance in these periodicals.

CONTENTS

Merwin:

This must be what I wanted to be doing,
Walking at night between the two deserts,
Singing.

AIR

Still the snow flinging in all directions, seemingly least of all
Down, and I an island in the sound
Of all that smallness falling
                              The fields stretch out
Their silences, catch the sighs of a thousand times
A thousand flakes of frozen sky

Fathomless the listening here

Calmly lush the sweep of winging white

A listening like an animal's before the spring

A listening like the forest's own—   All trees
Receiving the word *sung*
        Brushed-off, off-hand, upheld
For the duration
                        Deep in a braid of listening

Shush—maybe a music only

Inside my ears, maybe a waltz in the sizzling chorus, the allegro
Of wind
Having snow to show for itself

Air's winter avatar visible, its brief visitation on earth

Rumi:

But it's not given us
to see the soul. The reed flute
is fire, not wind. Be that empty.

ECLIPSE

Once upon the day the moon
   overtook the sun
      and life on earth
included everything ever
   made of atoms
      and everything else
at all that mattered
   (animal stone
      cyclone bloom)
when tall trees' leaves
   were still new
      and small
and drooping leaving
   so much room
      for the strange
sunlight to move through
   (and it did
      the sunlight
stroked by a darkened
   moon like a hand's
      unbearable light
touch such that every
   thing in this world
      hushed and called
at once and for a while
   a dim twilight
      brightened
midday with a light
   so lit and drained
      it rang

with something not unlike
   the ringing
      light
of truth
   we didn't know
      till then
we'd been longing for)
   and this leaf
      stilled
and this stone
   upturned and
      singing
and this space
   sighing
      with relief
as the outline
   of moonshaped
      glyphs
glowed and waved
   on the pavement
      beneath leaves
(a time frame
   created
      of light
and collapsing
   the distance
      between planets
and the interval
   between night and day)
      and all
manner of other things
   changed

and charged
with the light of insight
    until light's
        own language
spoke in tongues
    of leaves
        to the land
illuminating
    shadows where
        there were none
and always
    in the shapes
        of crescent moons
because the moon
    made moonlight
        of the sun
that nightly gives moon
    its own light
        until the sun
(passing down
    its sentences
        to those of us
who dared to stare
    at the ground
        and there
to find
    some filtered
        essence
of patterned light
    embracing
        the pantheon)
drew such a chiaroscuro

such a brilliant
shade
of light oh
there was a light
that blinded
us to rounder
suns of brighter
days!

HEARTS

THE BOY

That night, it was full
like rainwater. They danced
but he wasn't sure how she felt.
All the small things
poured down. Having never flown,
never kissed anyone he didn't know
since birth, he forgot
the distances to lips,
forgot himself: the edges ran. All night
it seeped so anyone could see
the humid air. And still was full.
Who knew how like rain
it could spread and not adhere,
how his own shape could not
contain its weight, such heat, the vapor
like a living fog outreaching,
that the aching fullness
could loom so empty,
hunger with no mouth.

THE GIRL

Had it happened yet, what happened those times
she'd swear she heard the echoes
of slow pianos beyond the trees,
she would have remembered that then,
would have taken him there one day

as she later took the others and remembered this:
the first time another's heart struck
across the layered landscape of cloth
against hers, beneath it a vast open place spinning
within her waist's small circumference.
Not till much later would she recognize
that certain diffused focus familiar
when it drew from her as if by force
of one private gravity all the fluid
most often at rest inside. Even then
she was a well, but there was not yet a meadow
far up in the hills where finally the hammering
of untempered strings would fill her
with the liquid of impossible musical rain.

HEARTS

Had it happened that time it was full
of echoes like rainwater? They danced
to slow pianos, sure as trees.
All the small things remembered then
poured down, taken, one day flown.
He'd never kiss the others.
Since the first time birth's heart forgot
distance, lips' landscape
was her's: the edges of a vast, spinning night.
Within her, its circumference seeped
still, humid air, till much later
that rain—diffused, familiar, new—
adhered:

the gravity of private fluid shaped.
Inside: the wait, the rest, contained. Vapor evening
the meadow she was. They reached into a well
achingly full of a far hammering.
They strung their loom, emptied and tempered,
over the mouth of music's liquid hunger.

COAST

       If as one we raise our kites to where they splash
into the blue
       ocean of sky each paper-and-wood diamond's
long neck
       a vine that swings and climbs
a stem that betweens
       and if they entangle
curl one string in tight
       design around another a danger that might strangle
but if instead
       every time beautifully the calm choreography
unleashes their lassoes
       at that height if they let the moderate winds
necklace and spread them
       open wide if unlooped my kite
in a smooth movement
       washes through that loosened knot like a wave diving
in a ring of rock
       if it leaps upward freed into all the diamonds
flashing where the frothing
       surface swallows up the thousand strings
of one sun's
       floating light and then reflects it back

DISTURBANCE

I will be the rock, igneous, fast to the place
where the river rips apart around it
if these blurted waves are its song

A pride of angels balances on the head
of a single aria that breaks around me
like a fire that's pleased to eat itself, the air

So I will sleep in this slow-burning house,

in its mouth, so long as the smoke of skin and pine,
brick and fur and cloth and food boils and flowers
by me like steam off October ponds

Split open a honeycomb over the nail of my tongue

Then see me be the beech for no reason
collapsing back into the bangled embrace
of maples, into the extended time

it languishes there in dying You come upon it
after years, and all the years that pass behind you
press you on more quickly, a compulsion

riveting as the need you are powerless

to appease There's no other way to see the light
but splintered through obstacles that plunge it into
the pied colors of all those windowed vials

in apothecary shops So let me be
the drunken bee by the compost
puncturing the sweet pulp of rotten apple,

enraptured now beyond the logic of pistil and pod,
sputtering on in the damp shock of sugar, if I can
be trapped that happily in the painted tunnel

I blaze with my own bright sting.

WHITE ON WHITE: A LANDSCAPE

Cricket wind in a paper cage
        Circling
                Full garden under frost
Sphere of unbreakable glass
    Daylight down the well
                Songs without words
What we travel through to move at all
    What we move when we travel
             Empty room
That ancient craving for the sugar
                Of ripened berries and sap
White on white The indivisible
        Once invisible
                  Shattered into sight
Perilous storm to perish in
    Or a wedding quilt
                Warm from love
           First forbidden glance
At last at an unfractured light
Its color Its name
             Ghosts galloping by on clouds
              Nightmirror
To fall through To float because of
                To breathe in
Braille Untouchable
        Six doves in the snow
             One eternal ellipse
    Ice dam Landslide Avalanche
Ashes ashes
Black crow Walking

AFTER MARC CHAGALL

BRIDGES

Painter to the moon to me. Canvas to stone.
To each his own lunacy, if lunacy be what art is.
Bridge circle to cone. Bridge steeple to road.
Layer the homes and farms over the dried paint,
shine of the new dependent on the old
as lovers *(to each other)* rest upon bouquets.
Allow the colours of the past to show through
like *windows to paradise to revolution to despair.*
Bridge marriage to mourning. Bridge up to down.
Cow to rooster to town, and *wings to the ground.*
Take what you are given *(bridge shoe to roof,*
bridge red to blue) gratefully, and describe it
in the moment before it falls *(to another)*
and imagine it standing still, turned around,
upside down. *Lines drawn to the faces,*
head over heels, heads over tails, feet
in the clouds. Many and dizzying and true
to the heart: All the world's inner
interlocking arcs, all *bridges to beginnings.*
If moon or aqueduct glow, reflected in the sea,
who's to say which is water, which is sky?
Floors of firmament like so many
stories on which to stand, stories to suspend
disbelieving from. *Annunciation to Elysium.*
Tallis to crucifix. Aurora borealis
to the night. Take the slip of blue canoe
to the avenue of strings, from dark channel up

into the musical sky. *Within to without.*
The hidden to the mind. Paint the invisible
from every side. Bring *detail to the myths.*
Life as it really is: this wondrous circus
of oddities and beasts, *the dream's illusion bridged*
to the real, miraculous to murder to absurd.
Reversed and reverberant with multiple mimed
conversations between things. *Ears to the eaves!*
Eyes to the witness! Will to the whim to imagine!

BELLA

In your topsy-turvy world where the houses
          hold still on their own roof tips, shifted
like a woman's skirts as she turns to leave,
          where candlesticks fly with a whip and a scythe,
light shatters down, triangulated, every time
          of day intersected in blues and grays, in shades
          above the graves. An archway
through the fence to the stones. Black veins
          on the leaves. Now the woman looming
unforgettable, summer thundercloud woman
          too large for this world. Her downward look
a sad one, or else the kind of watching
          that leaves the face a blank: a frozen brook
          whose waters still run underneath.
You want to reassure her she *is* there, brush
          against her dress dark over the sharp
          hedges of shrunken forest.

In the clearing below, her child, faceless, plays.
          You step away from the easel to hold her
          small hands and dance.
Maybe that bird needs a ladder to climb
          to the topmost branch of the sky—
but not the woman who is loved like this,
          who can balance above buildings,
nor the violins rising up in rays from the river: alms
          for a god who has tampered with gravity.
You play their heart's strings, their bird's songs, their
          Orphean grief and everyone
          wants to rise to that sound
and lie with her in the clouds.

UPROOTED (1941)

And where can we live now?

Not in the shtetl under the towering elm,
nor on the outskirts where once the hens

grew large as love and moths were drawn
to Sabbath candles. I thought you could wear

your white dress forever, to lighten
the bluer feathers of the sky.

Or that we could rise, still grounded,
like the Eiffel Tower, like fire in the clouds,

on the wind of your blue fan, darling,
landing everywhere with our bouquets and books,

our farms, our music, and our prayers. Darkness
instead has gathered before my eyes:

Look how the storm clouds writhe
behind roofs: How will angels pass through?

Every day that lilac glow to the west
spreads the sunset with gunsmoke.

Those homes we leave but never leave behind
will grow tall, but not before

they fall to ruin in war. We will not be safe
though we walk across waters

to a new world. Inconsolable.
On my palette the paint

dries to the pallor of winter,
of memory, black exhaust and ash.

BLUE SOUL

It might be that the cow would surely
bend over backwards
like any brave acrobat (which she is not)
to kiss the dark
side of the moon, with which she is in love.
Her blue milk arcs
across the skies, sparkling and cool.
It might follow
that the rooster would crow up toward her,
remind her

of her four pliant strings
and her bow.
If only she had long fingers, and a voice
less inarticulate, less low,
then she might sing. If only she were less afraid
of the coming down,
then her heights might mean more joy.
Her great white mass
spirals, backlit by her love, who in turn is sparked
by another.
The air feels dense enough to support her
like a globe:
She uses it as resistance, as a womb
against which to move,
amniotic element more feasible than fluid,
more breathable now,
and as tangible to her, and safe,
as solid ground:
No, more. Her greatest fear not the spinning,
not the fall,
but the landing and the breaking there,
her heavy bones
disconnecting from themselves inside her skin.
All along,
a single eye on the eastern side
of the old barn
must see why she hovers above like a star,
like a love story
never told. The barn's own hayloft bays
with desire for her.

Its wooden roof, with moonlight on it, might
hold her weight;
sometimes she thinks she might settle down
—or at least sleep—
there. Instead she croons her musical prayers
to the moon,
its craters still just heaps of stone and dust
like the hills
of Jerusalem where prophets lie buried
upon prophets
who remember when they were lifted and spun,
held aloft like ordinary
children, tossed and caught and tossed, knowing yet
only the thrill
and not the danger of release.

THE GIFT

When I decided to jump, first I waited at the door
of the buzzing precipice, for the wind's hand

to stroke me, brush me, make me give
way like an avalanche. Already,

in that high plane, I could hear the opaque hum,
the om of the world becoming.

I thought I might be like that sound,
bursting my own stillness and birthing

my own self, I might be the shout, like Joshua's,
that shattered old Jericho's walls.

So, one leaf, I broke into the open
book: I entered the hourglass and began

to sift down the vertical corridor of my fall.
Once a man leapt from the 84th floor, suicide story

of the Empire State Building, and the updraft
placed him, almost gently, onto the ledge

of the 85th. For reasons of my own, I did not change
directions. I fell like a long strand

of pearls, slipping. I fell like a row of faces down
a totem pole. Soon I thought I was a circle,

a wheel, the emptiness that loves the cup the way
identity loves the mask: for visibility, for good

measure. I thought I was
a sensation on the wing, or a golden string

unskeining through the straightened maze
of my fall. Then I lifted my umbrella

inside the house of air and my heart slowed
to the weight of a feather on the scales.

Once, giving birth, able and one
dividing and still one, I thought: I can do this,

this pain is all mine and I can take it; I want it.
I was calm. Maybe I knew, too, I was screaming— .

So it was in my fall. The silence
I knew there, of the willingness of pure air

to hold me inside it—for once, for a while,
for now—was unspoiled by any terror

borne on the wind of my voice.
And I, finally, took flight: I knew it

at the last moment before I landed,
when a tiny moth, fully formed, flew up

past me from some last unknown place between
the ground and me, and because afterwards,

when I laid my body down, something inside it
kept on floating and turning in the sky.

SHED LIGHT

Snakeskin spiraling like flute music
    through almost blue air,
dim mosaic of tender spun glass:
    window upon window
its little panes of color particular
    as Arachne's tapestries.
Landslide of silk down creature's back,
    finished, perfected: sloughed.
Twisted shaft, lithe, feather
    light: no heft, no shadow,
no use but to be left
    to memory, a once-filled shape
unfilled, outspilled, watery.
    A dream of a body:
transparent now as what it housed.

SHAPESHIFTERS

On the opaque glass of the lake, layered over the clearer lakes
        of past and future seasons, a stipple of seagulls
            spelled the surface from shore to shore.
At first frozen, in one multitude they suddenly rose
        like smoke, then died down again,
            resettled in new formation on the ice.
Once again they erased their array, rising, reconsidering—
        then alit, statuesque as if sure now.
            Each sketch they made
etched the plain of their page afresh—
        as if to say: this; no, this; no, *this*. In my vision,
            words flickered in air without speech,
burning to carve from the obscure a visibility:
        grounded, the words took shape, sculpted, all at once
            defined as birds. Marvelous geometried
creations of sense—one by one everywhere I saw them
        whirl into wheat stalk, spin into street,
            mottle, flex, and flare
into oak bark, ash branch, blackened maple leaf.
        Now the quiver of images lifts and falls
            like fire in the stove that is the same fire
from fall to spring, even though the only constant is
        the feathered glow of heat,
            and even though each ax-hewn log
I feed it is unique. Each shivers the flame, holding its own
        brief wing against the cold, like a stone
            shifting shape against a chisel in flight.

THE LEAF

birch leaf under snow, on earth, the air
draining out of it, going sheer through it.

birch leaf thinning to transparency under snow,
snow melting, air lifting cold water, air

sucking more moisture from the leaf. earth
drinking some too. leaf as a part of the surface

of earth, a small fine horizon
between soil and sky, itself

part soil, part sky. leaf immersing, leaf
immerging, delicate, with earth. leaf dying,

tatting to skeletal lace, leaf tracing
its own insides. I think it is a window

now, to peer through to below. I think it is
a slow burn in the cold early spring

layer of time, I think the waters of spring melt
carry the ash of it invisibly

to the other side. leaf seepage.
leaf absorption. leaf passing through a solid

to another land, like a girl leaving
through a mantel mirror. leaf concentrating

days and nights like eyes
attending hard to the dark's dark shades.

see the apse of leaf's earlier curve
flattened to the lune of land, disintegrating

in the summer heat.
peer into its shadow self dissolving beneath its breathless

weight, its breathy weightlessness. air
pressing leaf down, earth soaking it in, leaf

compressing, nestling ghostly
between the elements. earth taking it in

as if reaching up to embrace it. air
giving it up, relentless. fabric, curtain,

dress, rag, scrap. new leaves
fattened by rain and fanned

to flame fall touching
earth around it, patches on the place

where it once fell. galaxies of cells
exchanged like partners in folkdance, atoms

in alchemy. birch leaf under snow,
on earth, the air

TO THE BONE

One against the other across
the fleetingly infinite field:
that dry crackling of pallid
corn stalks clacking comes close to it.
behind them mountains range like steppes
between the tiers of fog they coddle.
it's autumn coming close
again and you need to compare
this one to autumns past, recall the other
sputters of color too good to last.
something you need to say, something
you come close to:
wind in its limitless visits—
especially in fall when it cleans
the overblown trees—
wind in possession of you
says it best. but you go on anyway,
trying to pen the breeze:
this fall phenomenon different
from summer's in its macabre
celebration of the lifeless,
in its forever rewritten memory
of what comes next. sorrel
leaves swirling in a whirlwind
mimic your own compulsive
repetition, its own circle
of yearning so close
to a kind of comfort.
quickening conversations

of geese flocking south
chill through your thin skin:
behind it a choir of silence
undefined rows you
closer to what you'll never forget,
what you almost remember
this time. closer to its name.
the heart overtaken. the bare staves
waving at boughs' ends, the musical
red wings: something
they almost say, more like a sense
hunched in darkness, an ache,
a suspicion: every time,
closer to it, closer. hear
hard light on the hillside
flatten the visible scale
into two dimensions, and you're in love
with the flatted third:
the way it breaks you down,
over and over, to mean you are
alive. the way you rub it in
the wound that you never
come close to wanting to close—
as if you could scrub away the whirling
of everything else and come down
like snow to the center, the eye, so close
to the purity of knowing inside this
present pain, that searing
white place without wind or words.

NO WITNESS

Saw the constellations
  boil in the dark and then
    the partial moon in day.
Smelled the blown smoke
  of leaves bridge dust
    to sun. Saw the steep
wash of rays
  overflowing haze and soon
    an uncanny color calling
in the valleys. Saw the one
  endless mobius of mountain
    ranges overlapping, spilling
into seas, saw the grace
  of islands skimming there.
    Heard the echo hammering
of wings in the currents,
  a trilling above the keys
    of November trees locking
light into thin air. Saw the long
  shadows shouting
    ahead of time,
the smallish opening
  from which the foxes peer.
    Took the swarm of the cold
wind's bees on the face.
  Heard the breath of snow.
    Saw all word clouds hang,
thaw and rain
  what they had told on the road
    of names that frays
into fields where graves
  empty into earth
    and any witness yields.

THE OWL

If it can be called staring when no eyes are visible . . .
I thought I could wait staring back till I could see

some glassy feedback or glare of light in the socket
indicating reception, recognition, retina.

No wonder, for some, the owl encountered
presages a death: its eyes look

as if from the dead—all soul, or none at all,
it's hard to tell. It was a trap, a trick, the way

I had to crane my neck up, while it faced me down
from its perch with its empty eyes, its round

dark holes for eyes, till I glanced past it to see
if forest blackness was what came through its skull

from behind. It slid its own neck slowly
all the way away from me, its head with its cannily

judging eyes swiveling like mockery,
and then, deliberate, the face swinging back.

Caught at the brink of woods as if guilty, and it
a thing of weight and judgment, a beauty, a boast.

Cold blew through me at the thought of its swoop,
even more at the memory of its sound

like sudden coyotes howling, or like the sound
midnight might make falling

before twilight. And at the question
of what it saw in *me*, craving up at it, as at the last

desire of the damned. Of course
it was the first to let go, before I found any answering

light reflected in the place of its eyes, deep there
in the feathers of its cowl. And as it turned upward

and flew, with my new trove of religion in tow,
the fear and awe I never felt for God

nor ever knew the sense of until then, skewed
all laws of perspective in the heavenly

way it grew larger in expanse of wing
and wing, still lifting

my eyes along like an undercurrent
below it, the ground for once gave out

from underneath so that I was like the condemned
standing for one impossible instant above the collapse

beneath his shoes, the noose still limp and loose,
the neck expectant of its clasp.

GOD'S BODY

All for show, to win a point for their god
they put the bomb on the bus for a ride
    each miracle of god, each passenger, destined
for a small greatness at the next stop: that bareheaded
    man going home with only bread
        the teenagers meeting after school, the lonely
and the lovers in a tiff all of them of a piece
    each a piece of their god then the crashing metallic
        spectacle, with audience participation:
                look—that man's hat
blew off, a pale crown and its ragged red brim, the girl
        raising one finger to point, surprised, and that
too, flew   all of them now farflung, a farfetched
    patchwork strewn, all their clothes and concerns
               to the wind   god
    they had no fair warning they'd be a part
of this light show, it was
    their last dance, their last act of letting go
skull cap unraveling, wave of a kidskin glove
        eyeglass flashing, one foot kicked
    fifty feet high all flesh of god's flesh, blood
of god's blood, scattered like a dozen tribes
    like a diaspora, the women and the men
at odds, the still unsculpted children, the sundry
        spry and the miscellaneous infirm
    the unhinged, the angry, and the ones at peace
watch this, god, these pieces of your body
        split, goddamn it, spin crimson and sink dead

like leaves and twigs in a real windstorm—a true
act of god, watch them rise and fall like hope
godgiven, like noble ideas and causes
godforsaken, like nations, indivisible, divided
under god.

WORD
(after the Kabbalah)

Word, you are the story
buoyed upon the tones of your own boat,
that which sails ahead of the wind
at the brink of speech.

You are the shape, the definition of being,
who manifests the invisible, who draws it
into life. Every sound of you
a totality innocent of the whole

which changes in everchanging
rearrangements of its selves.
Each sound of you an infinity
of sounds which together are the sound

of all that is sempiternal.
Each sound an icon, an eon, the mouth
of forever, each sound the source
of another and the origin

of silence.
Every letter a witnessing
angel of god, power, beauty.
Your alphabet

measures me, weighs the size
and form of every thing,
numbers the possibilities
of possibility.

You name the names
of the earthly, you are the entities
that, uttered, form it.
To contemplate you

is to behold the holy,
because you are its name
which is itself the thing.
Word, you are the pollen

that coats the cavities of air
everywhere, and catches in my throat.
In your light I see what you mean
traveling like shadows alongside you.

You are the indelible pitch
of pine that rubs my open palm,
the pungent and surrounding
musk of skunk—

a scent that stings my eyes,
that soaks my skin,
that hits me like a hand, an essence
I inhale

like the first
piercing breath that all at once
with a cry
filled me with life.

FRACTURED LULLABY

Before we broke in two like old continents in the sea,
when you formed the shapes of the moon
below my ribcage, a pangaea, you breathed
like the silent swimmers undersea.
Tonight a solar wind inflated the moon
until its light
so filled the sky
it pushes now against the bones of our brook,
against the windows, and your mouth:
You tried to say the moon
rose like a skull, that it wanted to steal your breath.

Canticles of air
reel through the bare trees, runneling
through the branches' tiers
as if romancing a higher wind . . .
But all is still, more still than a hundred held breaths.
Large and white, the moon
runs stark striations like reefs everywhere,
as if a lost land made of purest light,
now arisen, is returning to night air.
Every color's consumed in this white,
a great arcing collusion with the moon.

Between your interrupted attempts to breathe
I hear that moonlight spatter the spaces
between things, stinging like blown
snow, unhesitant at the horizon,
spilling unnatural blue, liquid ice . . .

Out there, fluid, the sky is singing its air.
In here, each finished breath,
crooked, broken, or—mine—crooned, ripples
in the room. All this moonlight:
blackmail. All that air,
of no use to you here, enclosed, at sea.

In this visible zenith of light
I stare at you, amazed that you curl outside
of me, that we have split apart like a sea
of cells, like atoms, like a harsh exhalation
forever leaving the throat.
I want to beg forgiveness, to say
only that giving birth is the breach
of a promise, the good flood
letting up, leaving you self-contained above water,
poised, precarious on dry land, under the moon,
requiring air . . .

I can't keep you afloat.
I can't keep that oath of harbor,
or breathe for you your breaths.
But light steps over the threshold: see
its breathable air? See how the sky—
in any strange or ordinary light—
falls to its knees at your feet, so lightly,
even as it stays aloft?
You whisper, Listen—do you hear the sky?
I answer yes, but it's the sound
of your effort to take it all in.

IN SUMMER NIGHT

Not a distant
   urge, nor a far cry, but *here*,
inside, real as what she hears herself
   say, this far flung hum of airplane
as it rips through the open
   skylight: same way moon eclipses
beneath thumb, sound's touch
   drowns out sight's,
defies perspective—the object out
   of reach but its proximity
certain in the ear: intimate
   company, color, flash, heat
and scent: a sting to the wrist,
   skull bone shift, salt on the tongue . . .
now the string suite of grass loud
   in her crown, no knowledge
of shrieking unseen insects
   to dissuade her sense from pain:
curled hands like wings fly to her ears,
   not to shield them from intrusion
but to wrench out the already
   mutinous within . . . small child,
too attuned, a conduit not yet
   accustomed to skin or limit,
still horizonless:
   everything enters in—*is* in,
hitched at the heart to the vast
   and vastly true . . . so that in her room

the mosquito, that invisible brush,
   repaints her darkness silver blue,
outstripping the walls
   of their shadows' speechless hue: so
another winged nail tears the static
   silk of summer night,
renaming the air
   hot blanket, panic, song.

STARTING SMALL

Amidst such violence as the sky's
with its unshielding cracks, its unwieldy enormity crashing through
and lighting up our bones
amidst its steady, ongoing, thrumming, unrelenting forever
drumming rain, its laughing erosion of skin and lash, of wooden deck
of river bank or garden edge, of tact
how do the lilies
even the little alyssum
remain sloping upright
neither cowed nor overturned
by such a tumbling downward
of whipping water and wind?
Or the birds unquestioning under their wings
or the squirrels merely paused between two seeds—everything standing to meet
the outcome, the downpour, unrepentant, unafraid?
The rains rope downward
the rains all swing
on the guffaws of air. Alight with random flashings of fire, the raining
air explodes, abstract element
transforming into sound and sense beyond
magnetic fields, electric forces, the friction of heat on frost, of clouds on high.
In the doorway, envious at the threshold, I will myself
to lean upward into it, like a stem to enter up
into its need to plunge on down
its utter love of release and repeat.
In fact the wild frightens me, although I choose it
although, wet, I step onto the floating grass, catch
my hair on the darkened bark

of trees that at any second

> could split at the seams. I am only human

and falling hard from heaven to earth

> the teeming sky

> > is too much air for me.

I want to start again, small. Tonight

> after this storm passes over

let's heave open all the sodden windows and doors
let's switch on the electric lights

> one for each room at least, and host

the afternoon's damp aftermath of moths and gnats,
the siren song of mosquitoes wanting only a taste

> of what we hold inside, the silent tune of bat food

> > in search of warmth and salt: their simple greed so pure,

their fragmented plenitude like rain's abundance scattering;
let's listen to their ping and preen breezing in the halls

> and pattering on lamps, the din of insects negotiating

the plausible distance from ceiling to floor—so little

> they ask of us really, so little we're willing to take.

GEOLOGIC TIME

Almost daily
  for a decade I have passed that bog.
      Once a lake, its shallow bottom
        unseen beneath dark water
was rising in an effort
  to meet—halfway—the air. Now,
      between two greens, a single still stream
        winds through its center—
but none of it will hold
  weight of more than lily pads or wheat,
      though the brown mud's suspended
        like some medieval alchemist's dream.
Rich, damp, defined
  by the slopes of drier forms that surround it,
      the marsh plies into meadow over
        geologic time, treading
its own waters
  until they begin to close in,
      complex with all that's befallen:
        it takes that long to become.
Beneath summer's heat the marsh stretches,
  dead stumps and branches bleaching
      like the bones of steer
        on another ancient expanse.
Weeds rust, roots soaked
  in their saturated home.
      They have had to make of themselves
        their own terra firma

to stand themselves upon:
   each wet blade of grass sustaining
          its small ball or wing of seed, dying
           to make its own bed, to drop
into its own decay. Like this
   the landscape changes, each rippleless
         touch to the scum
          one leap
toward solidity, toward soil. Finally
   the grass stem falling, afloat, adrift
         on the surface of its history, a raft
          for its own next self
to raise a sail upon.

EVOLUTION

Devoid of summer light's device, stripped of chlorophyll,
don't the leaves reveal their true nature,
their mute green equanimity exsanguinating

as each one plunges—in a many-echoed collision,
choral, multiple—plunges into fire? All for one

and one for all: infinite witness fractured into bits.
Rivulets of color occurring everywhere
like the currents of color in the very air
similarly invisible until prismed. Unaccountable!

What the eye disbelieves, doesn't the mind see by refraction:
dumbstruck doubletake, sidelong glance, the way we look
askance—beside the star—to see the star?—

Or think we see: for don't we see instead the long time dead
and darkened, a mere spatial memory appearing
as revelation, a sudden flash of insight

into light? Weren't we caught by surprise in clarity to find—

between lake and sky, in a perfect fit—*this* pattern knit
in black and white spells "loon," each feather with its exact
spectrum of spots and stripes well placed: and all about
and spreading out from its smooth movement of loon

the water stipples into slimly ribboned strips,
reflecting the loon's own fluid lines, and the lines
of lowering early-autumn leaves and light . . .

OLD DIARY

Dark and airless there until opened, after eons—
no one having recorded the slow change since, though change
is all that has ever occurred: Cavernous place, ancient gaping rooms so long

invisible and buried and in a timeless, unimaginable, unwitnessable dark:
An old diary no one keeps, unoccupied chamber where rock casts no shadow
as it grafts onto its slick-wet shelves,

where stone itself flows like water
only slower. Solid, but stippled as if by the same flicker
as wind over ponds, those low waves

stay for ten thousand years, while still spreading. Until the shock
of being brought to light: Inside clasped covers, memories
you thought were fixed whisper like stalactites, slippery substances

of liquid calcite through the decades taking their own shapes,
separate from yours—whole series of new shapes forming one by one,
day by day, linked only at some lost source. Years later I might say,

Don't you remember how, in anger, I overturned
the table, spilling the tray, all its contents suspended for once
in the arc of their recollection?—but they are unbound

by any steady present past because no, in fact it was you
angry at me, *you* who pushed the table, or in truth it was neither, only
we both said we would, or thought it, and now remembrance blames me

for writing it down as I must have believed it to be and then reshaping it anyway,
unwittingly, year after year, never looking it up, never looking back.
And all the while there has been a force, a spiral, the very birth of a life,

continual flowrock piling itself on and upward

from a single opening and spinning out of the ground

that lies in darkness underground, stalagmites in the cave.

No one enters that place. Every hundred years, if you could return,

you'd notice more small growth, more rivers sculpting that sluiced stone,

more liquid rock shifting, dripping, in secret, though nevertheless

holding up the world we know. How shaking, then, to discover the sexual pace

with which the familiar became strange. So that when you say

that I am still the same—whatever can you mean? Who was the one

who lived that life, there, in my own handwriting? Look how,

since that time, it has poured like glaciers down the hard walls

of its pages, scrawled in the dark through niches of clawlike rock as if desperate

for a toehold, sculpted itself daily with the imperceptible elemental blades,

time torn. Now these sharp, fluid forms exposed: Beautiful, frightening, so unlike

anything I ever knew or thought

I would remember.

INTERIOR WITH PAINTER'S WIFE

She is a model wanting
        only a touch
                of light. Cornered
   she stays inside,
        and though large she barely figures.
Inside / outside / beside her
   all areas surrounded by / overlapping /
        engulfing another and she
   always a part / apart / entrapped.
Why does she stay?
Paneless windows open to somewhere
           she no longer wishes
      to go / only a tiny place
inside of her
        to prevent her from escape.
Oh it could be so easy!—all those openings
      he's laid out precisely
           so that only the edges
of the pictures themselves shut like doors against
        sight / imagining /
   the unpainted rooms of her life.
Planes of light that glide so casually
      over the sills idle
         at her feet / illuminate
   the shadows of dulled longing / the fact
of the *elsewhere*. Is it more beautiful there?
      Less still / less clean? Does light less
   blithely turn corners and slip

across surfaces, mocking?—
the bright ocean, too, threaten to lift
    its skirts / skip
            over the threshold there?
The simple statement of her
            nude body in the barren room: nothing
    against the ground of space and light
            he brushes hard against it.
Her passive stance becomes the positive
            counterforce opposing
                    open air / the best position
    from / for his perspective.
Do you see her / him?
Even in the sullen / unseen interior of her
    thoughts—no mobility /

FROM SOME NOTES ON LONGING

Light rain strokes home with slow arrows swooping

The luna moth waits, wind-pressed to the screen

Dark trillium pinwheel unseen beside the deep woods ferns

A dusty perfume leaks like lust from buds

Fetal, the leaf curls, its flesh devoured by snow

White stones, small grey skulls, all wet, shine

An old husk opens in a time you love but can't recall

One low branch lets fall its fruit, soft, swollen

The clarity of black soaks the bark of oaks

Above it all, the sky begins its closing from within

Grass parts imperceptibly for the last swallows of rain

AGAIN

In weather this cruel, we haven't got a prayer
for rain. Even that moist bed under stones
where scaled creatures curl in satisfying dark—

even that safe place evaporates and *again* is an old stone
turned over. Last shrapnel, lost potsherd of Babel turned up
in our own backyard.

For so long tucked under
forgotten mud where the wistful leaves kept on dying,
yearly burying themselves as if out to reinvent the earth.

Parched stone story, like a book pressed openside down,
and the ground reading it, stunned: letter
from an old love still capable of paining. Moonstone shard, darkside

now exposed to light. I stayed clear
of the woods in windstorms: fear of blindness in the thickets
slapping at my face. I stayed clear of the open where gales like harsh silence

close in more darkly than arms. Like the deer against the stone
wall, I am a creature of edges: edge of longing, edge of danger,
edge of change, of death. But this tripped me up: rash edge

of rosetta stone kicked up from the dust
like mail delivered by simoom. Now it falls to me, lies heavy
in my hands. How do you put it back, take back

what the wind said, puzzle out like an unpleasant clue the errant stone
in the shoe. Because now all the pieces overlap—their precarious edges
won't snap into place—hard angles frayed. Sharp bedrock, surfaced.

Last word, fossil. Pollen hurled from the flower
of the cactus that blooms in the desert only once
in a hundred years: the language of wanting, finally spoken,

has a heat, a clarity akin to air's. Through it fly bird call
to bird, wolf howl to wolf, his pleas to me flashed across the currents
of hot magnetic space: *No, not again. Don't say another word.*

SCISSORS

Having split apart, though still attached at the heart,
like scissors, now only one direction exists: In.

But the two sides gleam across in separate
glares of refracted light, threat
to every creation and labor, every effort
at construction: Stitches, string, glue or loom, what binds
parts together into one—
                                        and scissors
are mirrors, fragmenters, tools of simultaneous
division and increase. One into two, two into shreds,
threads unraveling until ragged, slivered, frayed.

Still, I have this vision of halves healed whole again,
the split needs slid back together, coming to one point.

But most dangerous of all, most chosen,
seems the closing in, that one sweeping way to meet—
most frightening: Once begun, inevitable? That act
of going—from open to closed, from separate to joined—
a repetition of stiff fingers curling into fist.

And this indecision, also, breathes
the words of the king: It is fair, in place of agreement,
to cut the thing in two. Into two wrongs
                                        the scissors split
and across the gap each blade hisses its unique loss,
each loss greater than its reflection's. Think

of those shining surfaces, their sharp edges
nestling easily, plane to plane, safe. But between

the click and the clack, the this and the that,
the doubling slash of the one hand greeting the other—
does more destruction lie there?

Before the finished fold, surrender, that single point
of view—first the puzzle jigsawed, zigzagged,
disconnected and discarded in the clap
of stainless steel rays slicing, slitting
sheer through their own twin arguments

with whatever comes between them?

SWEET VEIN

(watching the comet in March, maple sugaring season)

Breathe in the trail of its light, ice river vaporizing
from light years afar and melted from the spilling dipper . . .
Now taste this: a water bathed with the sweetness
rising, released, the sweet abundance of stars instilling dark
with its white sugar grains . . . Boiling, boiling,
all night the smoke billowing milkily, clouding the cold
bellows of snow, the breathing below freezing after a day's
bright thaw . . . Dark, darker, the syrup
darkening under midnight's departing moon: the comet
moonlighting, the sap—moonshine . . . Come dip
your long-handled cup across the eastern branch of sky
into this steam, into this stream of liquid dust sailing
through the open vein: a splendid suspension to sip
at lips dark and wet, to raise up, drink in, swallow:

HOMING

Be there at dusk when hawks
cross the clearing.
                    In the smallest thing
                    live smaller things
            unbreakable
as atoms used to be:
                    things unknown
even in the intimacy
            of what is
                    at home.
Stoop to the strange
            transparent
            hair-like worm
that piers off a stem
in the garden wet with rain.
                    Be surprised
                    be lulled:
            both.
                    Stay
for when the child
remembers fathering you.
            Stay in one place
            for a very long time.
            Marry it.
            Move in not on.
Until nothing
could be better
than this
        (every)
                    instant—
                    nothing better
than this love

this body
this weather
    with all
        its inconveniences
        and change.
Get microscopic
    the object ever nearer
        to the eye
        expansively.
Be blinded
by the nearness
    and then wait
        for new sight
        returning.
Not to know or to own
        but to see:
your vision unclouded
by the far by a need
    to go there someday
        sucking *this* day
        from sight.
Desire *this.*
Savor *this.*
    Not other
        not new
but always
        in the same
the otherwise
the renewed:
    sameness surrounded
        by enough air
        enough silence

and you.
           So that you hear it
when the deep groan
of the planet's momentum
           pushes the unheard-of
closer to your ear.
                   Listen closely:
dust settles
into new fractals
crystals
           of soil
                   taking their places
                   with an infinitesimal
                   hiss.
                   And look:
One leaf
trembling.
Sunlight
           unbalancing it
                   spilling
                   over its edge
falling
           there!
                   into your hair!
Did you feel
                   its kiss?

DEGREES OF GRATITUDE

It was given me to be grateful for the branch,
how I got to see it day after day as if intentionally
placed on that steep rock, center-stream, in spring—

for an ordinary branch, two-pronged, long, and of a size
for brandishing in an angry hand—and more,
for how unreachable it was by any hand

and for the tall gray rock softly splitting the run
of the water, and for the water itself so hard and fast
it was a force that, rising, could lift a broken limb

out of and above itself and place it soundly upon a rock—
yes, and for the same water so gentle that falling
it could leave the branch, leave forever without bearing it

over to the other side . . . even more for the balance
of nature that moves the eye to attend to a branch,
inert for days on a rock unmoved by rapids: so wonder

must be a thing that can flow upstream, so that as the river
becomes the other rivers moment by moment, the moment
of wonder remains in the stream.

TROMPE L'OEIL

Truly the bunting is three birds, even if seeing is believing.
Magic act, thing of beauty, the plain and simple
truth. For consider the angle of the light
as it falls upon uncolored feathers, imbuing
them with the chance to be iridescent blue,
to be flat brown, to be seen clear through.

Look at me in a different light. Because

this is not about the vision that pierces its target,
nor the canyon into which drops the distance
between observer and observed. Not about how to see
beauty or the lack of it, or your own mirrored self. Instead
beauty and its lack, beauty and its loss,
absence—all the same—call at once from the seen,

in spite of you, your solitary point of view. Simultaneous

alternatives arise, regardless of what meets the eye.
Possible parallels: the reflection, the sheen,
the lackluster lay of overlapped wings. Take me,
colorless and perceived by you, the sight of me emerging
beautiful from your eyes.
Just so, the bird "looks" blue but it is "not,"

just so, the plumes reflect the light and give it back: Renewed

for safekeeping in either eye or sky. And the air, in its turn,
from all the colors chooses only blue to offer up to you,
till the skies fool your eyes into that one unwavering choice,
every other conceivable hue hidden behind that careening blue.
Simple illusion of a blue not really there at all in the bird,
nor really all there is in the sky:

I want you. Endlessly

eddying flight of color
fall for me and I will let you pass through
like light riffling indigo feathers, and I will absorb you
into my lightened, windy bones, and I will reflect you
like highlights off the wings of the requited, for what else
would I believe in, in place of such lustrous lies?

AFTER SLEEP

Slipstream of daybreak at rooftop.
Sky so newly deep in blue it drew down into it
            all life, centrifuge, spinning,
diurnal, like the birds rising, birds falling
in the name of light. Birds flashing their feathers
            in their own wind,
indistinguishable from the other
wind, sky spirited away and into them.

Up the slope of dawn, a dark flock
      of stars in daylight—starlings—banks
         above, a shock of cloud turning
            as one bird,
         turning now into the sky
and vanishing: invisible like that on one wing,
angling back to discernible on the other
      like blades flipping from flat to edge,
         from plane to line, over and over
or like a crazy earth in rapid revolutions
      of dark and light, dark, light.

Each westward swing of the birds against light
         when again they disappear
      is like the sun's flight, like last night
         when I told her the sun falls forward
            beyond sight. I told her
it's not gone, honey, only taking
the long way home, and I only sleeping
      in my room. I said *don't be afraid,*

night carries day in its wake like an anchor,
　　and even if dusk seems like an end,
nothing ever comes to an end.
　　　　Bright thing: She didn't believe me.

Faith's other name is habit: the sun's own
　　stationary crawl over the world again.
　　　　Or birds on the sky like a paper boat
　　　on another current, moving like this
and like this, the way she dances now in daylight, fearless
　　　　because the sky came back.
　　　　But then the birds
curtain away in a flash
　　of air, just air—
　　　　all that dawnlight a sleight of occlusion
　　　　　　on the other hand of night.

　　Spinning, circling, the birds dip into the stirred
　　　　cauldron of dawn and dissolve . . .
　　　　　　　then, soon, slide through the sliced
　　still point of amazement, and spill
back to birdness visible: overflown light
　　　　lashed still with spokes of motion
　　　to the rock of the planet, once more
　　slipped back, like a mother
　　　　　　after sleep.

CLAY BABIES

Gardeners of March, a brown flower in every palm.

O holy water and sand, transformers
of seasons and small children
with their yard sale kitchen tools and hard dolls
turning mud into cake, poison soup, quicksand, camouflage.

And they meld down into it, slopping their little snow pants
into the molten sculpture pinned with pine needle,
insect wing, remnants of robin's egg, turtle shell, and rain.

Pirates and archaeologists of goo,
they follow maps of worm journeys to the treasure trove
of glittering mica shards, shed exoskeletons, half disintegrated
golden leaves. It's the invisible airs that capture them,
hold them hostage, enchanted. It's those pluming gulps

of last summer, last spring, in the last breaths of fall
this ground sucked in before the cold spell cast
in ice and snow had them pocketed—it's that warmed air
now posted as ransom notes: because from the earth's sap
liquifying, now that breath blares out calling

to children newly stretched and yawning from winter and dark
afternoons: *Party invitation, rising yellow balloon,
buried doubloons and clay to mold! Come on out and see
what you can make of this!*

GENERATION

    Counterclockwise, spiraling stems up
their guides with triplicate leaves alongside,

    tracking the trajectory of daylight's daily
victory over the rein of gravity,

    the vines of green beans climb: drape
a loose one leftward toward its support:

    in its own gentle tantrum it twists away,
backs off, acrobatic: serpentine, insists on scaling

    space, sparring, trailing the slow cycle
of the sphere that spins its rise . . . offspring,

    compass, time traveler: curvature that turns
as the North Star to the pole, turns now against it,

    each fresh vine surpasses the finite: arrow
arcing airward, oblivious of its roots earthbound.

ANTICIPATION

Under many moons the field's surface ripples, mimicking
the way age shapes its waves on skin, loose footing for a crow.

Through the days and nights since seeds were handed down
and lowered under ground, in silence but for the wash of wind and rain

the slight and grassy shoots balloon upward and out until they're thick
as bamboo. Each kernel's fine umbilical cord will be joined to the other

gathered into a single tassel of silk that pours through the slim opening
in the corona, the husk a papery origami folded over the ear

of corn inside. Above, tall red clusters will lift their lashes
starward. Beside the rows of growing shafts, beyond the edge

of the field and the season and the ripening, and under the denser
shade of trees and under the spell of yellow, silver, green, stalk

the raccoons, who wait all year, year after year, not knowing
that they do, not remembering what they're waiting for,

but knowing that they want it.

DEVOTION

Under the invisible celebration of green and small spiked
fingers, spread, delicate, flat and curved like flame

Under the tender stems indented like the one deceptive wheel
of the unicycle designed for riding the high wire

Under the rim of soil in its raised bed, the horizon
of soil that skims and covers the protected and the hidden

Under the weather, under pressure, under our own soles,
the cooled carrots fatten—

                      after all this time of clinging

To the source, their soft color's lifted off the earth, their cling
so easily loosened with a single circular twist

And then in that moment, and then, for another moment,
                   the dumb, intimate dirt

Embraces the shape of the carrot, embraces the place
of its absence in the ground

KILLING FROST

What arable light there still is gropes low
to the ground, under cover
like an offshoot, the stolen

meant to root a next year's round of growth.
in search of more airborne light
the lake lifts off:

each wet plume of ice, as it rises, wrapped
inside its own white web, ghostly
as the visible articulation of the unsaid

in final warm breaths exhaled.
yesterday still alive

in red globes, green bells,
the garden begs to differ, loves
to die like this, instant crinoline
under the skirts of curtsied clouds.

this morning the sky hard as tombstone
to break, hard as your word, I thought,
when you promised to winter it through.

what's different is this: the whiff
of sleight of hand, no second wind
handed down, an air too cool
to be hoodwinked by any frantic fall

of old leaves coming true
at last in their own light. lake light,

like feathers played on the air
of a reveille. or like what hangs
in the balance. now I see in hindsight's
headlights that riveted look
gulping off your face saying what

I'll never know. oh.
frozen over. no follow through.

like these blue winds: daydreamer chaperone
who looks the other way, idiot chauffeur
driven by the dying light.

RAIN

When the sky shoves in   flashes past
        our shoulders for one last look   loose ash
like fertilizer in our fists
sticks to the creased designs of our skin   aging
        the life lines and this rain
won't let up   reminds us of you
          won't even let fall away
the soft fine soil left of you
        but changes it once again
so it sifts through our pores a pewter mud that molds
        like wet clay to the shapes of us
filling half moons of fingernails   half healed wounds
        trying to take form in the half shells
of our curved palms. *These are our hands yes*
         now let go let go!
        Arms drop to our sides or rise into the rain:
where do we put our hands   do we wipe them
        tacky with wet ash on our skirts and pants
or on smooth leaves whose seeds
          you once planted here? Soak them
like stained cloth in sudden puddles by the road
hold them out to each other   more mementos?
        Gesturing helpless we surrender:
This rain will dry again and leave us too
        in the dust. Now it breaks us open
        the same way you said rain
breaks open earth not sky. We feel the grey
        lines trickle and drip past our wrists

up to our elbows like picnic juice

let the rain

laugh at everything   wash us clean   sweep

the last of you in rivulets right through us

on through veins that pulse out to a sea

climb out like Venus and descend again   we promise

we'll try to recognize you.

MISSING

like paper cut-outs the part cut out
the part left behind to hold its shape

like shadows on the floor the seemingly distinct
forms of things not there

like the deceptive edge of sight where fog
conspires to be wall like the other side

where things again emerge smeared smudged
with some fine ash like the dust of moths

on your hands however much you meant
to leave no trace your fingerprints

all over everything fugitive with the powder
wings are poorer without

THE EYE

Darkness begins like trouble, world
closing in on the eye.
Oh but these diminished chances
change our dreams,
throw a last wheel of light
hard against the wall.
Or describe a child's ring
drawn in white on the sidewalk,
safe circle for the newest charm
that appears inside every night:
Ballerina. Lentil. Soldier, shell, rune.
Tiny rocket ship
taking off for your eye.
Take me up on it—I want to fly
into the center, time it just right
to pierce the clouds as they whorl
against the clock, enter the storm embracing
its own emptiness. What blinds me
tinctures the air in its turn: Dust
the funnel sucks up
into its circling:
Dust to dust: That is all
that makes it visible. Nothing
in *its* eye, nothing that hurts, no hunger
here for clues to any future
or its legacy. Easy. Only a cyclone
roiling upward a rotation of dirt
it will later release as rain.

Pendulous pirouetting sky,
        airy nautilus, rolling overkill:
I need the spinning house
of this wind, its secret room within—
        the lee between hillocks of blackened clouds
            is where at last I could slip
        to sleep, oblivious of the wild spiraling
beyond the closed eye.

STRANDED

When snow melts cold on my face, relieving the fever,
        and through the open window
I look in at my still body
          in the upstairs bed
I frighten myself back
        out of this last brief snowfall of spring,
          back to the dark
hot with crowded souls, the night come down its countless
        slender lines, razor-thin silks raining
the black spiders descended from the blankness
          above earth,
etched here as if by an error in the eye:
        inside, everywhere,
          the once-plain air now a substance
of spirits visible to eyes grown accustomed to the darkness
        inside them, a match of dark
and dark that sparks a different vision:
        the air a receiving tomb:
they are talking to me now, not quite in voices but
        in little electrical stars
          falling on me in soft flecks
and I don't know what they want
        to say, leaning in to me, a pressure on my breath,
thick as the blood that is thicker than water,
        whispering
like the low sting buzzing over phone wires
        that makes bears in the woods claw at the poles
          in search of the honey of bees,

all speaking at once
        like a low rumble or hum, a lightning storm far off
over the mountain, so I can't tell what they mean
              to say . . . and who are they,
all these souls, dressed in their dark
        clothes as if still following rules of propriety,
           who is the one
closest to my hair, her own of another era,
        her expression almost of love:
the room is a web, a lace
            of forms shouldering the spaces between
objects and walls, though the walls themselves are no boundary:
        unlimited even
           by pine siding, they continue on,
in quantity, on
        beyond
the night, through the snow in the humid season of my room
           and in the trees,
past where snow ceases, past its source . . .
        and why can I now see this,
           how the darkness in secret traces
the shapes of all these souls, why can I hear the air
        of their chorus, even begin to repeat aloud
the sequence of their song: they want me
           and I'm not ready:
they lift me in the network of their fold, carry me
        out along the road,
           faster and farther
than engines or wheels—
        past the miles of cord

strung and scalloped like musical staves sagging
                    above the earth, like broken
loose spiders' strings suspended from the poles—
            and into the damp morning sun,
              and then the lines are
the scaffolding for endless actual webs, the spiders—
            they are legion—taking the empty space
between distances, the miles
                  of girders support for the stranded
threads of their perfect design,
             and I am spinning in the sweet vibrato
                of the voices between the lines . . .

MAP OF A DISTANT LAND

I woke up most mornings above the clouds.

There, I waited for that white sky
to lift off from the river below me
and catch up to the air before my eyes.

Half the mountains were mountains
and half the mountains were clouds.

On warm wet summer mornings like this one

I looked across the two rivers, afterthought
of green between them, and the white
mountains that were clouds

rose from the darker, grounded mounds

then passed on through me, and passed
on upward like old souls heading home
at last, turning invisible, slowly, as they flew.

MOORINGS

We enter the empty field and mourn
   for shells those louvered origins
   homes smoothed by moving waters
     The places
inside unbroken Lost
in reverie beyond houses and
     adrift on grasses newly mown
   for hay palms a moment
at pause upon their blunt
   stiff tips rock them
in place Purple vetch alfalfa clover
   and rye whorl the breezes
     down distance buoyed by trees
     down across our legs
      carving curved horizons
   Still while all day the sun
     pours west its last streams
      piercing the evergreens the leaves
of the deciduous until light slants
     radiance a mirror
in the lit waves field almost
    afloat and now we are this shore
     we were never awake to before
     we and the hundred million
   spiders' webs aride the shorn stems of
interrupted meadow harboring
    sails raised upon
infinite masts
    webs webs webs spread expectant
   of small strokes dew seed
insects beaks us
    dust

Dogen:

There are mountains hidden in mountains.
There are mountains hidden
in hiddenness.

RELEASED

On its hind legs close before me the next mountain
is a dark bear rising as I crest this peak

morning sunlight sharpening the trees

the trees slicing their places into sky

then dulling with new red buds then smearing
the lines with full leaves . . . also the rain not falling

but sweeping up from underground
rivulets that raise their breaking voices . . .

the bear scaling the hillside, nails long
from slumber stretching across wet bark's

most ancient ring, harmonic . . .

she takes each new weed as it sprouts
into her mouth, holds it there soft as a cub, waits

for its slow spring spice to resonate

inside her taste:

and finally begins to suck

broadcasting its scent, pungent, splendid . . .

spruce and pine with yellow tips
lift the light at the edge of green

circled with auras of new growth . . .

I stay for every note, rippling, concentric

every verge and echo of a thing I can find releasing
while the grey paw prints shadowed
in the last pillows of snow become little blisters
and then whispers and then gone, stay until

the late day sun makes light blue leaves
until my skin is the same temperature as rain
evaporating off moss, when the sun ferries
over to the place where west turns down

cellar holes fill with the chords of dark balanced
on all fours

the bear's hunger quelled.

Alice B. Fogel's previous poetry collections are *Elemental* and *I Love This Dark World*. Her poems have appeared in many journals and anthologies, including the *Best American Poetry* series, Robert Hass's *Poet's Choice*, *Iowa Review*, *TriQuarterly*, *Poetry Daily*, *Ploughshares*, *The Journal*, *Third Coast*, and *The Bedside Guide To No-Tell Motel*. Recipient of an Individual Artist's Fellowship from the NEA among other awards, she teaches writing, literature (including a program on how to "get" poetry), and other arts for all ages. In a different vein, Fogel creates clothing primarily out of "reprised" materials (LyricCouture.com). She lives with her family off the grid in Acworth, New Hampshire. For more information, visit www.alicebfogel.com